IN THE QUIET CORNERS

MANSI UPADHYAYA

TO

MY MOTHER & BROTHER

Contents

Preface

In The Quiet Corners is a collection of poetry born from moments of stillness and introspection. It is in these quiet corners of our lives, away from the noise and chaos, that we often find the deepest truths and the most profound emotions. These poems are a journey through those hidden spaces, where whispers of the heart and echoes of the soul come to life.

This book invites you to pause and listen to the soft murmurs of existence that are often drowned out by the clamor of daily life. Each poem is a reflection of the fleeting yet powerful experiences that shape our inner worlds – moments of longing, bursts of joy, shadows of sorrow, and sparks of hope.

In The Quiet Corners explores the delicate interplay between solitude and connection, dream and reality, silence and expression. It is a testament to the beauty that can be found when we allow ourselves to be still, to feel deeply, and to truly see the world around us.

I hope that as you read these poems, you will find your own quiet corners, spaces where you can breathe, reflect, and rediscover the magic in the mundane. May these words resonate with your own experiences and inspire you to embrace the stillness within.

Welcome to the quiet corners. May you find peace and wonder here.

Love,

Mansi Upadhyaya

1. The scent of roses reminds me of funerals

I am a pessimist,

perhaps a bit too much.

Maybe that's why I find people unappealing,

their words like empty vessels

filled with promises unfulfilled.

Sunny days,

those grand deceivers,

mask the inevitable return of darkness.

Laughter, to me,

rings hollow,

a mere distraction

from the persistent weight of sadness.

Birthdays,

those annual reminders,

draw us closer to the end

than to the essence of life.

Quiet moments,

they are but the calm

before the storm.

And love letters,

oh, those fragile keepsakes,

they are souvenirs from a past long gone,

echoes of emotions that once were.

Each joy waits for its demise.

Each smile, a prelude to the tears.

2. Blue

Gloom settles in like twilight
creeping slowly across my chest,
I cannot figure out how
to get out this mess.
The only thing I know
is to paint it blue.
The canvas absorbed
all my silent screams,
in various hues.
I cannot face this labrinyth
so I paint it blue,
as I still seek the dawn
the only way out is through.
My days are stuck in december
but I yearn for may,
So all my monday blues
turn into greys.

3. Rains & Roads

It has been raining
since a few hours now,
turning the roads into flowing rivers.
I watch from my window sill
The onslaught as it continues its downpour.
I can hear a sweet hum
almost hypnotic,
coming from each raindrop.
As if beckoning me to come out.
To get out on the roads,
and drench myself in the rain.
I close the window tight,
to stop my heart's flight.
For I can't step out now,
Not yet.

4. Daylight dreams

In mid-afternoon's embrace,
I find myself washed
away by the tide of dreams.
Harsh edges of the world blur,
I wish to slip through the cracks.
But something still anchors me
firmly here.
A friend named
procastination whispers
promises of escape,
Tasks pile up, bricks in a wall
around me, deceived.
In the corner of my mind,
desperation lurks,
A scream for everything I dream
sweeter air, skies so wide,
fleeting visions, grasping harder.
But the clock ticks loud
Tick
Tick
Tick
It brings me back to the tug-of-war,
caught in limbo, prison

of my own making.
So I sit here,
welding my own key
to be someday free.

5. In the wake of you

It was a whirlwind, a hurricane,
I started to fly-
My wisps of hair and
your locket tied
Bedsheets on the floor, but us in the sky,
Until we crashed and I turnes to blue,
And there's not one scratch on you.
"Is this what happened to us?", I said
You found someone else
to love instead.
I screamed at the mirror
And broke into pieces
You closed the door as the shards pierced me,
And I drowned in the pit,
of my own blood and defeat.
Oh, how the tables have turned!
From you saying, "you'll find someone"
To me asking "Did you find your 'The One'?"
Ashes of polaroids,
of moments I kept,
I stayed in the room
for months after you left.
not knowing why I was shunned

I burned the midnight oil,
till the air turned to fumes in my lungs.

6. Conversations are poems

Late afternoon shadows
fall across the kitchen table,
he asks,
"What do you think makes a poem?"
My fingers trace the rim of the glass,
eyes lost
in reflection,
"Moments," I say,
"captured in the net of language."
I whisper,
"Do you think words ever rest?"
The coffee cools between us,
steam like thoughts that rise and vanish.
"No," he replies,
"they breathe through us,
each syllable a pulse,
each pause, a heartbeat."
Our hands meet,
our fingers lace like rhymes.
We sit,
the evening settling around us,
"Do you think," he starts, then stops,

"that silence is part of the poem?"
"Absolutely," I whisper,
"it's the ellipsis,
the unspoken truth."
Our hands rest together,
a couplet against the day's prose,
a dialogue unfolding
in the hush of twilight.

7. Contradictions

If you like me, don't talk to me.

If you think you like me, stay away from me.

If you like how my eyes shine when light hits,

you should see how they drown in their own sea.

If you like how my hair trickles down and frames my face,

you should see how lifeless it is.

If you think my laughter is contagious,

know that my sadness is too.

If you admire the way I stand tall,

you should witness the weight that threatens to crush me.

If you like my words, how they dance and play,

you should read the silence between my lines.

If you see the glow of my evening's face,

you should glimpse the shadows that haunt my dawn.

If you think you know me,

you should know that I'm pretending it all.

8. Tales of a Hundred Books

I have a hundred books
in front of me,
hundred worlds to dive in,
Each one different than the other
one's gold and the other diamond.
Some witches and wizards
some dragon slayers,
I'm everyone of them
Even a lover's prayers.
Pages whisper secrets
of lands far and near,
tales of triumph,
and tales of fear.
Each chapter a journey,
each word a spell,
lost in the stories
where my heart does dwell.
Adventures unfold
with each turning page,
a timeless escape
from the world and its cage.
In the silence of the night,

under the moon's soft glow,

I lose myself in tales

only dreamers know.

For in these hundred books,

a hundred lives I live,

a thousand dreams

that words do give.

An endless tapestry

of wonder and lore,

each story a treasure,

an open door.

9. Coffee

All my days
coffee all alone,
never looking down
note on the door,
waiting to be picked up.
I meet people
and promptly forget about them.
You must be angry
But do you think of me?
or am I just a speck of dust on the beach?
I'm swiping people
left and right,
But I don't like my hand held tight.
So I go back into my hobbit
Pick up that note,
and have coffee
bittersweet,
all alone.

10. Tell Me

Tell me you don't like me
Tell me I'm bad
Tell me this is not what you wanted
Tell me this is the worst you've ever had
Tell me I'm a waste of time
Tell me I'm boring
Tell me I'm a thorn in your flesh
Tell me I'm not worth exploring
Tell me I'm the storm that destroys everything
Tell me I'm the rain that floods
Tell me I'm the sharp dagger
that only knows to draw blood
Tell me I'm the missed beat in your favourite song
Tell me I'm the shadow on your light
Tell me I'm the doubts you can't erase
Tell me I'm the reason for your haunted cries
Tell me I'm wretched
Tell me I'm forlorn
Tell me I'm despicable
Tell me I'm forgone
Tell me Tell me Tell me
Tell me everything you hate about me
Maybe then I might stop loving you.

11. Fall Of Rome

As I see the bleak walls
that once stood heavy and tall,
Ruins and tatters of everything
who knew even this would fall.
Empire's night descends with
echoes of glory that now fade,
betrayal whispers through the cracks
of stones that werre once great.
Senate halls now empty
Barbarians at the gate,
A storm of chaos brews
Each left to their own fate..
Ancient ashes now dissolved in the river
Empty halls, where now ghosts roam,
Empire's lost and battles won
It's still grand, the Fall of Rome.

12. Smoking kills

What do you think?
what happens when we smoke?
Does it go into our heart?
Does it go into the dome?
or does it just take us under,
beneath the layers of our home?
My friends said "you need to cough it out"
You need to tough it out.
All the voices with the puff,
said it was a hoax,
And it will never not be true.
I know smoking kills
So does loving you.

13. City lights

When I was running my hand
through the strands of your hair,
Golden auburn, you looked
like a greekgod there.
Do you see the lights
of the city street?
It looks like something
out a painting where
only we could meet.
That night is still in my
memories
like a faded headlight of a taxi
like a screenshot taken by
my eyes,
That painting is still on my wall
which listens to all
my whispers and sighs.

14. Drafts I never deleted

Did all I could
everything for you,
Emails that I sent
but never got a reply to.
I did everything I could,
to remove you from my mind
burned everything down,
until there was nothing to find.
The only thing I never defeated
were the drafts I never deleted
In the hopes that someday,
this story would be repeated.

15. The Art of Giving

I can't stop giving,
even when I know nothing returns.
When I like someone,
I can't help but give,
each meeting a new offering,
What will they cherish?
A bracelet, flowers,
a curated playlist or just goodbye?
Do they even notice?
Do they even care?
Questions circle like vultures.
I don't think they do-
they don't appreciate the gifts
or me.
I expect nothing,
yet I give,
because I don't know how to stop.
The act itself consumes me,
like an endless well,
a habit formed in the shadows.
What if I paused,
held back a moment?
Would they see me then,

in the silence of my stillness?
But I can't stop
the compulsion too deep.
Giving is all I know,
and perhaps,
all I'll ever be.

About The Author

Mansi Upadhyaya, the author of the book you've just read, is about to start her Master's degree in Molecular Biosciences at the University of Bath. When she's not knee-deep in science or writing, she's either crocheting like a grandma on caffeine, obsessing over Taylor Swift or building virtual people in The Sims 4 (where she assures us, her digital alter ego leads a much more organized life). Mansi's hobbies might make her sound like a 19th-century artisan and a modern-day gamer rolled into one, but hey, who says you can't mix molecules with a little bit of mischief?

www.ingramcontent.com/pod-product-compliance
Lightning Source LLC
Chambersburg PA
CBHW032004140726
47988CB00019B/3340